# THE BULLET

# THE BULLET MANAGER

---

*Getting down to what really counts
in the workplace*

PAT KAUFMAN

CINDY WETMORE

ARROW
BUSINESS BOOKS

First published in the United Kingdom in 1994
by Arrow Books Limited
Random House, 20 Vauxhall Bridge Road, London SW1V 2SA

Random House Australia (Pty) Limited
20 Alfred Street, Milsons Point, Sydney
New South Wales 2061, Australia

Random House New Zealand Limited
18 Poland Road, Glenfield
Auckland 10, New Zealand

Random House South Africa (Pty) Limited
PO Box 337, Bergvlei, South Africa

Random House UK Limited Reg. No. 954009

ISBN 0 09 939331 X

Printed and bound in Great Britain by
Cox & Wyman Ltd, Reading, Berks.

To Dick: For his creativity, objectivity, tenacity, patience, and love.

To Jake and Haley: For being very special, for keeping their mother humble, and for their love.

PAT KAUFMAN

To Dan: For his support, patience, and love.

To my father: For my ambition and drive.

To my mother: For her unconditional love.

CINDY WETMORE

# CONTENTS

Introduction    xi

Anger    1

Assertiveness    3

Assertiveness – Barriers to    6

Beating the Blues    8

Body Language    9

Brainstorming    11

Burnout    13

Buzzwords    15

Change    17

Conflict Resolution    19

Corporate Culture    21

Creativity    23

Customer Service    24

Decision Making    26

Delegation    27

Difficult Irritating People (DIPs)    29

# Contents

Diversity Awareness   32

Ethics   33

Fast Shots   34

Feedback   36

Firing   39

Getting Along with Your Boss   42

Goals   44

Gossip/Rumour/Grapevine   46

Hiring   49

Humour   52

Image   53

Image – Body Language   54

Image – Dress   55

Image – Handshake   57

Image – Voice   58

Information Flow   60

Interviewing to Get the Job   61

Keeping Up to Date   64

Leaders – Traits of   65

Listening   66

Management by Objectives (MBO)   68

Managers – Good Ones   69

Meetings   70

Memos/Letters   73

Men/Women at Work   76

Motivation   80

Names and More   83

Names – Remembering   85

New in Charge   86

Office Decor   88

# CONTENTS

Open Door Policy   89

Orienting the New Worker   91

Performance Appraisals   92

Power   94

Presentations – Before   96

Presentations – Effective Writing   98

Presentations – Giving   100

Presentations – Reducing Anxiety   102

Presentations – Tips   104

Profanity   105

Project Management   106

Promotions – How Never to Get One   108

Sales   109

Sexual Harassment   112

Smoking   114

Stress   115

Stress Management   116

Success   118

Suggested Reading   120

Teamwork   121

Telephone Tips   123

Time-Saving Tips   125

Time Thieves   127

Total Quality Management   129

Traits of a Good Employee   131

Unions   133

Acknowledgments   134

# INTRODUCTION

Busy, successful people have little time to read long
   books.
The high points are what most of us remember
   anyway.
This book is small, streamlined, and direct. It is
   intended to be kept on your desk so it's there when
   you need it – NOT at home in the stack of when-I-
   find-time-to-read books.

# Anger

It's not the anger, it's how you express it.

Anger quiets people, builds resentment, and stops information flow.

Never, never, never lose control.

Act, don't react.

Don't kill the messenger.

Write it out, then tear it up.

Decide what your goal is. Will expressing your anger help you reach your goal?

Follow the 'two-minute' warnings (wait at least two minutes before you act):

- Calm down. (Breathe in calmness and breathe out anger.)
- Ask: 'What could the consequences be if I express my anger?'
- Ask: 'Will I burn any bridges?'

'Will my anger get me what I want?'
'Could this person ever be my boss?'

*See* Burnout; Feedback.

# ASSERTIVENESS

Assertiveness is taking ownership for your thoughts,
feelings, and actions without blame or apology and
accepting others' thoughts, feelings, and actions
without blame or judgment.

Some differences between passive, aggressive, and
assertive people:

| Passive | Aggressive | Assertive |
|---|---|---|
| Shy | Pushy | Forthcoming |
| Apologetic | Accusative | Clear |
| Insecure | Forceful | Calm |
| Afraid | Domineering | Secure |
| Unsure | Reactive | Active |
| Guilty | Controlling | Responsive |
| Quiet | Negative | Positive |

The handshake:
  passive – limp
  aggressive – bone crushing
  assertive – firm
Eye contact:
  passive – downcast
  aggressive – stare
  assertive – direct
Walk:
  passive – shoulders slumped
  aggressive – watch out!
  assertive – head up, assured
Language patterns:
  passive – I'm sorry, I should, I'd better
  aggressive – you should, you'd better, you're not
  assertive – I prefer, I will, let's discuss, I believe, in
    my opinion
Listening:
  passive – always very quiet
  aggressive – impatient, interrupting
  assertive – interactive, attentive, and responsive
Talking:
  passive – talk very little
  aggressive – dominate conversations, loud
  assertive – clear and direct
Response to frustration:
  passive – self-blame
  aggressive – explode and blame others
  assertive – clearly express feelings and frustrations
Others respond to passive people by ignoring them and

to aggressive people by being fearful and angry toward them. People feel that assertive people are approachable.

Assertiveness – How To: the following are the keys to changing from passive or aggressive to assertive:

- Increase self-awareness.
- Be willing to change.
- Be willing to initiate.
- Show a willingness to confront and resolve.
- Have a willingness to negotiate.
- Demonstrate a willingness to listen to and consider others' opinions.
- Be willing to take ownership of your own behaviour and point of view.
- Be willing to ask others, whose honesty you respect, how you are perceived.

*See* Change.

# ASSERTIVENESS –
# BARRIERS TO

IF YOU THINK YOU CAN, YOU CAN;
IF YOU THINK YOU CAN'T, YOU'RE RIGHT

The following are barriers to changing from passive or
aggressive to assertive:

- Putting yourself down.
- Apologizing excessively.
- Crying at work.
- Losing your temper and control.
- Acting childishly and helplessly.
- Giggling nervously or crying excessively.
- Poor eye contact, body posture.
- Tag phrases such as 'you know', 'okay?' 'kind of'.
- Excessive perfectionism.
- Stubbornness.
- Hedging with comments such as 'I might', 'maybe',
  'I guess', 'kind of'.
- Inability to accept compliments.
- Avoiding conflict or always being a peacemaker.

......................

- Excessive need to please.
- Excessive guilt.

*See* Difficult Irritating People; Image.

# Beating the Blues

FEELINGS FOLLOW ACTIONS. CHANGE
YOUR ACTIONS TO CHANGE YOUR FEELINGS

Do something new.
Indulge yourself.
Take a walk.
Call a friend; talk it out.
Write down your feelings; keep a diary.
Exercise.
Have a massage.
Read a funny book.
See a funny film.
Watch or do your favourite sport.
Meditate.
Have sex with someone who cares about you.
Eat well; get plenty of rest.
Get outdoors in fresh air and sunshine.

*See* Burnout; Stress; Stress Management.

# BODY LANGUAGE

## READING BODY LANGUAGE IS LEARNING
## TO LISTEN WITH YOUR EYES

People believe what they see much more than what
  they hear.
Look for incongruities. When words and body
  language don't match, believe the body language.
Be aware of what your body is saying.

Confident body language includes:

- Taking up space. Arm over chair. Sitting back.
- Firm handshake.
- Direct eye contact.
- Large arm and hand movements.
- Straight, erect posture.
- Brisk, assured walk.

Weak body language includes:

- Limp handshake.
- Hesitant eye contact.

- Slumped body posture.
- Excessive or nervous smiling.
- Nervous gestures.

Common body talk:

- Crossed arms – defensive, closed.
- Sitting on edge of chair – anxious, ready for action.
- Head nodding – listening, a signal to go on.
- Vigorous head nodding – strong agreement.
- Hand over mouth – undecided about what to say.
- Rubbing chin – in process of deciding.
- Jaw or hand clenching – anger.
- Shifting in chair – bored.
- Leaning forward – interested, attentive.
- Looking up – visualizing ideas.
- Looking around – checking for approval.

See it. Read it. Believe it.

*See* Assertiveness; Image.

# BRAINSTORMING

**BIRTH BY COMMITTEE SHARPLY
DECREASES THE PAIN**

Define a concise subject for the brainstorming focus.

Set the mood or tone for the topic to be brainstormed.
If you're brainstorming for Christmas marketing
ideas in July, bring a tree and Christmas music.

You want out-of-the-box thinking so create an out-of-
the-box environment. For example, get your staff
to dress casually, sit on the floor, everyone wear
trainers, bring Silly Putty, etc.

Consider inviting an outspoken, creative person from
outside your department to bring a fresh
perspective.

Keep the group small (five to eight maximum).

Try to facilitate, not lead, the discussion.

Write all ideas down. Ideally write ideas on a flip chart
then tape pages up where you can all see them.

Suspend judgment. Don't screen or criticize any ideas.

Focus on solutions. Discourage dwelling on the
   problem.
After the session, decide on the most workable ideas
   and refine them.
Give the group feedback about the results of the
   session.

*See* Creativity; Meetings.

# BURNOUT

OCCURS WHEN YOU'RE STRESSED TO THE
POINT WHERE MOTIVATION IS DESTROYED

Signs of burnout are:

- Increased isolation, negativity, agitation, physical complaints or mistakes.
- Decreased energy, attention span or enjoyment.
- Uncharacteristic emotionality.
- More excuses.
- Reduced problem-solving ability.

Causes of burnout are:

- Too much stress for too long.
- Powerlessness – that is, having little or no control over what happens.
- No-win situations.
- Too little to do or repetitive, tedious tasks.
- Multiple conflicting demands.
- Delayed and/or no rewards or recognition.

Prevent burnout by:

- Frequent praise and rewards.
- Practicing good time management skills.
- Learning to say no.
- Setting realistic goals and priorities.
- Taking time off for yourself.
- Letting go and delegating.
- Taking one issue, one project, one day at a time.
- Developing a variety of interests outside of work.
- Maintaining a good diet and getting sufficient exercise and sleep.
- Laughing.

*See* Goals; Stress; Time-Saving Tips.

# BUZZWORDS

Benchmark: A standard of quality to which other things are compared.

Cross-training: Training employees to do each others' jobs.

Diversity awareness: Becoming sensitive to, understanding, and valuing the differences (cultural, race, gender, etc.) of people so that each individual's contribution can be maximized.

Empowerment: The business concept of sharing power, delegating well, and allowing decisions to be made at the lowest level possible in the organization.

Flexitime: A system that allows employees some leeway in deciding their working hours: for example, 7:30 to 4:30 instead of 9:30 to 5:30.

Mentoring: Establishing a helpful business relationship between a senior and a junior employee to enhance the junior employee's career development.

Networking: Establishing good business contacts, both
within your company and in other organizations
and companies.

Team building: Motivating a group to work as a
cohesive unit toward a shared goal.

TQM: A management philosophy system founded on
doing it right the first and every time in the eyes of
the customer. Total Quality Management (TQM)
focuses on continual product and process
assessment and improvement based on solid data
and input from empowered and valued employees.

Value added: An enhancement to an existing product
in the eyes of the end consumer.

*See* Initials.

# CHANGE

Facts about change:

- Change is scary.
- Resistance to change is normal.
- Prior notification of impending change reduces resistance.
- Any change, positive or negative, is stressful because it takes more thought and energy.
- People value sameness and reliability; however, change sparks creativity.
- Even small changes impact the entire system.
- Fighting change takes twice as much energy as going with the flow.
- If you always do what you always did, you'll always get what you always got.

How to deal with it:

- Focus on one change at a time.
- Help employees see what is in it for them and how it will affect them.
- Explaining why change is necessary helps employees see the big picture.
- Whenever possible, include those key people who will institute the changes in the planning of the changes.
- When talking with your people, maximize the positive but don't deny the negatives.
- Even the best planned change can still stall. Make sure someone is assigned to monitor the change process and remove road-blocks.
- Help employees understand that a key to success is flexibility.

Stages of change/what to expect:

- Resistance.
- Discomfort, uneasiness.
- Assimilation. You start using the skill in one place/ situation.
- Behaviour transference. For example: As you manage and prioritize your time at work, you'll transfer those time management skills to other aspects of your life.
- Integration. The new skill has become a habit.

*See* Stress; Stress Management.

# CONFLICT RESOLUTION

Define the problem.

- What's the history?
- What's the current cause?
- Who is involved?
- What's been tried to resolve it?
- What are the obstacles to resolution?

Focus on solutions, not on the problem or the person.

- List three possible options.
- Look for win-win solutions.
- Decide on the least explosive option.

Take action.

- Bring parties together.
- Remain calm.
- Think, think, think, listen, and then do.

- Listen, listen, listen, and then talk.
- Define conflict as a mutual problem to be solved, not a win-lose struggle.
- Resist the impulse to take sides.
- Show concern and let employees put their points of view.
- Is this a battle or a war? Assess the consequences.
- Be specific about your expectations after the conflict has been resolved.

Common pitfalls:

- Ignoring the conflict; hoping it will go away.
- Jumping in too impulsively.
- Taking it personally.
- Minimizing employees' complaints. If it's a crisis to them, it will soon become a crisis for you.
- Assuming!

If all else fails, consider bringing in a mediator.

*See* Anger; Listening.

# CORPORATE CULTURE

SUCCESSFUL COMPANIES HAVE A
STRONG, DISCERNIBLE CORPORATE
CULTURE THAT EMPLOYEES CAN IDENTIFY
WITH AND FEEL GOOD ABOUT

Companies are value driven. You need to assess their values.

Values are basic beliefs about how business is conducted and how employees are treated.

Things to look at when assessing a company's culture:

- Company sayings:

  'We do it right every time.'
  'No one is irreplaceable.'
  'It takes every member of the team to do the job well.'
  'Our employees are our most important asset.'
  'The bottom line is cost effectiveness.'

- Rituals and traditions; such as company picnics, watches, retirement dinners, etc.:

How important are they?
Who attends?

- Image:

  How offices look.
  How correspondence looks.
  How employees dress.

- Heroes:

  Stories about successful people in the company.

- How are employees treated?

  Benefits.
  Profit sharing.
  Retirement plans.
  Personnel policies.

Job satisfaction is highest when your values and your
   company's values mesh.

*See* Ethics.

# CREATIVITY

Three-year-olds are quite creative because they don't
   know the rules.
Ask 'What if?'
Suspend judgment.
See problems as opportunities.
Capture ideas (even incomplete and silly ones). Write
   them down and keep them on file.
Challenge assumptions.
Let yourself dream.
Don't listen to negative people.
Seek out positive people.
Visualize.
Take risks.
Break the rules.
After creating, run your ideas past two or three positive
   people you respect.

*See* Brainstorming.

# CUSTOMER SERVICE

Customers want good products, good quality, a fair
price, good value, and to *be* valued.

The key to good customer service is to be easy and be
thrilling:

- Easy access.
- Easy to buy or check out.
- Easy returns, changes, or exchanges.
- The customer is thrilled with the experience.

Do what you promised when you promised.

First impressions are lasting impressions. You often
don't get a second chance. Image counts.

If you don't pay attention to the customer, eventually
the customer won't pay attention to you.

Indifference is the primary reason customers stop
coming.

Most customers don't tell you they are unhappy, they
just walk away.

Customers vote daily with their wallets on whether or not you will stay in business.

Never argue with the customer. Explain, listen, apologize, empathize, but NEVER ARGUE.

NEVER BLAME the customer. The customer is not the enemy. The customer is the lifeblood of your business.

Think of customer complaints as opportunities to improve. Be grateful and thank customers for taking the time to provide feedback on ways you can improve. Remember, most unhappy customers don't complain, they just don't come back.

Never take your eye off the ultimate consumer and who in your organization is serving that consumer.

You are either serving the customer or serving someone who is.

Whoever serves the ultimate consumer is THE COMPANY in the consumer's eyes.

Frequently step back, look at, and experience your business from the customer's point of view.

When serving customers, use their names and listen to their needs and wants. Individualized customer service is the key to good customer service. Everyone wants to feel special.

Remember, good customer service is not about pleasing customers. It's about thrilling customers! Positive word of mouth is your best advertisement!

*See* Sales; Total Quality Management.

# DECISION MAKING

Not deciding is deciding to do nothing.

There are no foolproof decisions. An amount of uncertainty is always present.

All decisions have an element of risk. The most successful people have made the most mistakes and view setbacks as challenges.

It is better to make the wrong decision once in a while than to appear indecisive.

It's usually easier to get forgiveness than permission.

Few decisions are written in stone and can't be modified later with new information and input.

The majority of decisions should be made quickly. The minority (high-cost, high-visiblity) should be made slowly.

Don't throw good after bad. We learn the most from our mistakes. When you make a mistake, admit it and cut your losses quickly.

*See* Assertiveness; Goals.

# DELEGATION

A manager's primary job is to teach and train
employees. The primary way to teach and train is
through delegation.

Eleven steps to effective delegation:

- Clarify and prioritize all activities that need to be
  done.
- Determine what you need to handle personally.
- Determine what you can delegate.
- Match the task to the appropriate person. (Caution:
  Don't burn out your favourite employee through
  overdelegation.)
- Provide adequate information and the big picture.
  (Tap into the need to belong.)
- Grant authority along with responsibility.
- Get agreement and commitment.
- Check for clear understanding of the task.

- Clarify format and time-line expectations.
- Let the employee know what you want to troubleshoot about.
- Share results.

The primary deterrent to effective delegation is fear of loss of control.

Each task delegated will prepare the employee for the next task.

*See* Decision Making.

# DIFFICULT IRRITATING PEOPLE (DIPs)

THEY AREN'T GOING TO CHANGE,
THAT'S WHY THEY'RE DIFFICULT

DIPs:

- Think of them as Difficult Irritating People (DIPs). DIPs in the road are part of life.
- All successful people have had to work for or with DIPs.
- Being able to deal with DIPs is a career asset.

Understanding DIPs:

- The key to understanding people is to understand what they believe in and what they're afraid of.
- Difficult people are usually scared, lost people. They don't have anything to be for, so they're against.
- Realize that some people feel so small inside they need to act tall and obnoxious outside.
- People who are controlling are actually terrified of losing control.

- Critical people are usually highly critical of themselves.
- Happy people are nice people; if you're dealing with not-nice people, you can assume they are not happy.

Strategies for Dealing with DIPs:

- Focus on your response, not their action. We get stuck when we try to change someone else instead of changing our part of the interaction.
- Make a plan for dealing with your DIP and force yourself to stick to the plan for at least a month. This way your reactions become automatic, thinking reactions, and not knee-jerk, emotional ones.
- Avoid making these difficult people the centre of your emotional life.
- Focus on work issues, not personality.
- There are two basic modes for behaviour: the THINKING mode and the FEELING mode. With DIPs, stay in your thinking mode.
- Take 'I' positions and not 'YOU JERK' positions when talking to DIPs.
- Keep your long-range goals in mind so DIPs don't sidetrack you into hazardous short-term emotionality.
- Don't give DIPs more attention than you give your good employees or coworkers.
- Keep a DIPs LOG. Writing out your frustrations will

help you stay calm and focused on the critical
issues at hand.

- Ask yourself:
  Is it me or do the DIPs do it to everyone? Does
  anyone get along with them? If so, how does that
  person do it? Would that person's method work for
  me? Do the DIPs have any strengths I could focus on?
- If all else fails, confront: ask DIPs, for example:

  What would it take for you to stop criticizing me?
  What would it take for us to work well together?
  What would it take for you to enjoy your job?

Goal-oriented people bounce over DIPs. They don't get
stuck in them.

*See* Assertiveness; Feedback; Firing; Motivation.

# DIVERSITY AWARENESS

## SEEING DIFFERENCES AS STRENGTHS

Diversity awareness is becoming sensitive to,
understanding, and valuing the differences
(cultural, gender, race, etc.) of people so that each
individual's contribution can be maximized.

Diversity awareness is being aware of and open to an
individual's differences without generalizing or
stereotyping.

The first step to working well together is understanding
and respecting each other.

Examine your prejudices. Look at your humour.

Actively seek out and pursue situations that expose you
to the diverse.

The reality is that your customers and employees are
increasingly diverse.

Those who succeed in the future will be those who
recognize, adapt to, and capitalize on diversity.

*See* Corporate Culture; Hiring; Men/Women at Work.

# ETHICS

Questions to ask yourself:

- Is this how the CEO of our company would do it?
- Is this decision in line with my values?
- How could this backfire?
- Am I burning a bridge?
- What is the corporate norm in my business? Is this illegal? Can I live with this?
- Will I worry inordinately about this decision?
- Do I feel OK about telling others about what I decided?
- Is this decision in line with my or my company's short- and long-term goals?
- Will I make a permanent enemy?
- How risky is this, and how much am I willing to risk?

# FAST SHOTS

If you never ask, you never get.

Decisions reduce anxiety.

It's easier to get forgiveness than permission.

Things usually are the way they begin.

Apologize, don't grovel.

If you keep doing what you're doing, you'll keep getting what you're getting.

Successful people have the most behaviour options.

If you're confused, ignore the words and believe the behaviour.

'A' managers hire 'A' people.

'B' managers hire 'C' people.

Negativity is contagious.

The solution is usually the problem. Change solutions.

When office anxiety goes up, focus on the work.

Do your job as if you owned the place.

Catch your employees doing something right.

If they were as good as you, they'd have your job.

Don't shoot the messenger, or after a while there won't be any messengers; you'll only get 'good' news.

What comes around goes around.

Sometimes doing nothing is doing something.

The laws of success won't work if you don't.

Never complain about a problem unless you have two good ideas about a solution.

Today's employee may be tomorrow's boss.

Enemies do come back to haunt you.

There are two kinds of people, takers and givers.

Yes, the world isn't fair.

*See* Suggested Readings.

# FEEDBACK

## IF YOU CAN MANAGE TO CRITICIZE
## AND PRAISE, YOU CAN MANAGE

Frequent, brief, immediate praise and/or criticism is
more effective than infrequent, lengthy, delayed
praise or criticism.

Think of criticism as 'helpful advice' to help employees
improve and succeed.

Don't procrastinate. Give immediate feedback at the
time the negative situation occurs.

Focus on the problem and the solution to it, not the
person or his or her attitude.

Ask for and listen to employees' ideas for solutions and
improvement.

Listen at length to an employee's response without
defending your position. The employee may need
to vent pent-up feelings, and you may learn
something you didn't know.

Stay calm. Adjourn your meeting and schedule a

follow-up one if either party becomes too upset or
agitated to discuss or listen effectively.

Be clear and specific about what went wrong and your
expectations for behaviour change. Get your
employee to buy into the idea and commit to
change.

Offer support, training, help, and guidance for desired
behaviour change.

Major in the majors, not in the minors. Ask yourself,
'Is this important or am I nitpicking?'

Avoid the 'but' tendency. For example, 'You are great
BUT . . .'. The 'but' negates the compliment so the
listener remembers only the negative.

Always use 'I' language. For example, 'I think . . .' or 'I
have observed . . .'. Avoid 'you' language, such as
'You should . . .' or 'You had better . . .' or 'You are
. . .'. You language causes defensive responses and
shuts down the ability to listen.

Praise in public, criticize in private.

Have regularly scheduled feedback sessions (quarterly)
with *all* employees.

Have job expectations stated in behavioural terms in
the employee's job description. This provides a
foundation for feedback discussions.

The four 'Fs' of feedback are:

- Factual
- Fair
- Firm
- Follow-up

If you fail to tell them they are failing as employees,
   you are failing as a manager.

*See* Assertiveness; Listening; Motivation; Performance
   Appraisals.

# FIRING

When someone needs to go, do it as soon as you can.
Tolerance of one poor performer can jeopardize
your entire staff's morale.

Two critical aspects to remember when firing are
*documentation* and *confidentiality*.

The firing process:

- Be completely familiar with your company's policies
  on firing (usually found in the personnel manual)
  and union requirements. If you have a personnel
  department, involve it as soon as you realize you
  have a problem employee.
- You will need specific documentation of poor
  performance over time. Document behaviour, not
  attitude. Also document time, place, and incident.
- Your primary concern is to avoid legal repercussions

and assure the firing is done fairly and for clear reasons.

Use progressive discipline. This includes:

- First: Coach the employee on what the problem is and how to fix it. If the employee claims psychological or drug problems, then he or she may be referred to the company's employee assistance programme for rehabilitation.
- Second: Issue a verbal warning to the employee that behaviour must improve.
- Third: Prepare a written statement to the employee outlining the problem(s) and solution(s) required.
- Fourth: Set a probationary period with close supervision and documentation. Make it clear that failure to resolve problems could result in termination.

The actual termination:

- Should be done in person. Consider how angry the employee may be. Do you need to have your supervisor or security present?
- At this point, in many cases it is wise to give the employee the option to resign.
- Be clear with the employee about the terms of the termination. This may include: severance package, outplacement service, what kind of reference to expect, what the publicly stated reason for leaving will be.
- Don't argue with the employee. This is not a time

for conflict resolution. If the employee cries,
continue the process. If the employee sobs, say you'll
leave the room for a few minutes to give him or her
time to regain composure.
- Time and place. The best time is Friday afternoon.
  The best location is in a neutral zone such as a
  conference room.
- Don't forget to get keys, computer passwords, etc.

Post-termination:

- After the termination interview, document exactly
  what was said and agreed to.
- Decide what and how other employees are going
  to be told. Confidentiality is critical here.
- If asked for a reference, most companies give only
  dates of employment and position held. This
  avoids legal problems.

*See* Hiring. (Do it right and you'll never have to read
this chapter again.)

# GETTING ALONG WITH YOUR BOSS

Make sure your boss has no surprises. Keep your boss
informed.

Never go over your boss's head.

Never disagree with your boss in public.

Never say anything negative about your boss.

Make sure you clearly understand your boss's
priorities. Plan your time and communication
accordingly.

Analyse your boss's style of management.

- Does your boss like brief oral reports, written
memos, or weekly conferences?
- Does your boss want you to drop in or make an
appointment?
- What are your boss's weaknesses – paperwork,
decision making, etc. Bosses are most critical of
employees who display the bosses' own weaknesses.

......................

- Does your boss expect punctuality?
- How flexible is your boss?
- What does your boss value in workers?
- How does your boss want you to solve problems?
- What pressure is your boss under?
- What are your boss's goals?

Adapt to your boss's style as much as possible.

*See* Traits of a Good Employee.

# GOALS

Your values determine your goals and your goals
   determine your priorities.
Set SMART goals:

- Specific
- Measurable
- Attainable
- Realistic
- Timely

Write down your goals. Writing goals down will
   dramatically increase your likelihood of achieving
   them. Review your written goals weekly and keep
   them in view.
Set both short-term and long-term goals. Make sure
   your short-term goals are compatible with your
   long-term goals.
Limit your number of goals and prioritize them.

Break down goals into implementable steps. Ask
   yourself: who, what, when, how, and why not?
At each step, evaluate your progress and be willing to
   modify the steps as necessary to achieve the goal.
Reward yourself at the completion of each step; doing
   so will help you stay committed to your goals.

*See* Change; Success.

# GOSSIP/RUMOUR/GRAPEVINE

NEVER criticize your boss or company in public.
Facts:

- All offices have gossip, grapevines, and rumour mills.
- Remember, the grapevine is often an early-warning signal.
- A highly active grapevine may indicate employees are:

  Anxious.
  Unhappy.
  Not getting enough solid information.

- Pay attention to open/shut doors. If you have an 'open door' company and you start seeing lots of shut doors, then there's a lot of gossiping going on.

Tap in:

- Tune in to the office grapevine. Ask several employees what the current rumours are.
- When you repeat something, never say who the source is.
- Never gossip about people's personal lives.
- If you want information passed on, give it to the biggest grapeviners.
- When people share gossip with you, always ask yourself: 'Why are they telling me this?'
- Tell your employees what you can that's not confidential. To get information, you have to give information.

Action:

- Improve the formal information flow.
- Don't take major action to squelch an inaccurate rumour unless you hear it from several sources over a period of time, and the rumour might affect company profits or seriously damage someone's career.
- Don't waste time trying to find the source. You may get a good idea of who initiated a false rumour, but it's rare to have proof.
- Manage by walking around. Ask people if they have any questions.

....................

• If action must be taken, try:

Using someone you trust to squelch the rumour.
Talking to a small group about the untruth of the
rumour.
As a last resort, issuing a written statement.

*See* Information Flow.

# HIRING

Before the interview:

- Develop a job description that lists all skills necessary to do the job exceptionally well.
- Review the job application to match the person with the job skills required.
- Develop a list of interviewing questions that elicit skill-specific information.
- Check references and read between the lines.

During the interview:

- Gain rapport. Use applicants' names frequently, and ask easy questions first.
- Listen more than you talk. Don't let interviewees interview you.
- Briefly describe the job and job expectations.

- Ask open-ended (who, what, when, where, why, and how) instead of closed (yes/no response) questions.
- Good general questions are:

  What would you like me to know about you?
  Why are you leaving your present job?
  Why do you want this job?
  What's most important to you in a job?

- Get skill-specific information. Present a hypothetical situation and ask how the interviewer would handle it. If skills are demonstrable, ask for a demonstration or samples of work.
- Ask value-related questions. For example: Whom do you admire most? Who has most influenced your career? Describe your best and worst work day ever. Who's been your favourite boss and why?
- Some topics are best avoided as far as possible:

  Age, or date of graduation
  Marital status
  Religion
  Race or national origin
  Children
  Political beliefs
  Military service or discharge status

- Give applicants time to ask questions.
- Thank applicants for their time. Let them know when a decision will be made and how they will be informed.

Deciding:

- Select the top two or three applicants and interview them again. Don't hire on one impression.
- Don't get caught in the need for a warm body.
- Ask yourself: 'How would I feel about working for this person?'
- Be cautious of the tendency to hire a clone of yourself. Hire for a balanced staff.
- Hire from within whenever possible – hire the known rather than the unknown.
- Don't ignore your gut feeling. Ask yourself: 'Do I like and trust this person?'
- In making your decision, remember, past behaviour is the best predictor of future behaviour.

*See* Interviewing to Get the Job; Listening; Traits of a Good Employee.

# HUMOUR

When in doubt, don't joke.
Humour relieves tense moments and reduces stress.
Most successful people have a good sense of humour.
Know your audience (even if it's only one person).
Learn your company's 'corporate norm' about jokes.
Never tell an off-colour, racist, sexist, or ethnic joke.
Never make other people the butt of your jokes.
Humour is funny; sarcasm is angry.

*See* Corporate Culture; Stress Management; Suggested
Reading.

# IMAGE

There are four key components of your image: dress, voice, body language, and handshake. All four must be strong and consistent to make a positive impression.

People make their 'first-impression' decisions unconsciously within the first ten seconds of meeting.

An efficient, strong image gives the impression of an efficient, strong person.

You should perfect your image so that it's not something you have to give conscious thought to. It should be part of you.

*See* Image – Body Language; Image – Dress; Image – Handshake; Image – Voice.

# IMAGE – BODY LANGUAGE

WEAK, INEFFECTUAL BODY LANGUAGE
CAN NEGATE ALL OTHER COMPONENTS
OF A SUCCESSFUL IMAGE

Posture should be straight and erect but not ramrod.

Seated posture should take up space.

Eye contact should be direct but not staring. Staring is
aggressive.

Walk should be confident, head up, and at a moderate
pace.

Smiling, when appropriate, always improves your
image.

*See* Body Language; Image; Image – Dress; Image –
Handshake; Image – Voice.

# IMAGE – DRESS

Always dress for work as if you have an important
    meeting that day.
Dress for the position you want, not the position you
    have. If you don't look as if you can do the job,
    you probably won't get the job.
Every company has an unspoken corporate dress code.
    Know it and dress accordingly.
Pay attention to the dress of the successful people in
    your company and dress accordingly.
Cleanliness, neatness, and fit are more important than
    quality and price.
Clothing should never distract from the verbal message
    you want to communicate.
Shoes should always be polished.
Women:

• If you frequently get comments on your jewellery,

make-up, or perfume, you're probably wearing too much.

- Nails should always be well manicured. If you don't have time to see to chipped nail polish, don't wear any.
- Avoid sleeveless tops.
- Build your wardrobe around classics that don't go out of style.
- Shoes should have closed toes and closed heels. Low to moderate heels are most appropriate. Tights or stockings are a must.
- The jacket is the most critical piece of business clothing. It denotes authority.

Men:

- Navy-blue and dark-grey suits are the most widely accepted colours with solid light-blue or white long-sleeved shirts and a silk tie. Shoes should preferably be black, and always polished.
- Socks should be midcalf or higher.
- Fingernails should always be well manicured.
- Well-trimmed moustaches are acceptable.
- Shirts should be crisply ironed.

See Image; Image – Body Language; Image – Handshake; Image – Voice.

# Image – Handshake

Limp = Passive

Bonecrusher = Aggressive

Firm = Assertive

Offer or extend the handshake. This gives the
impression of self-confidence.

Slightly step into the handshake. Again, this shows
more self-confidence than just raising your arm.

Always make direct eye contact as you shake hands.

Always offer your name as you extend your hand if
there is any possibility the person may not
remember your name.

*See* Image; Image – Body Language; Image – Dress;
Image – Voice.

# IMAGE – VOICE

You must sound as well as look important.

Voice is generally a greater problem for women than men. The business world favours deep, strong, low-pitched voices.

The key aspects of voice (with guidelines) are:

- Volume – moderately low.
- Pitch – low. Remember, the higher the pitch, the lower the credibility.
- Diction – clear.
- Clarity – always.
- Speed – Moderately fast. (People are more likely to listen.)
- Expressiveness – very.
- Tone – congruent with message.

Avoid: Mumbling, monotone, airiness, and nasal tones.

Punch important words.
Keep your hands away from your mouth when talking.
To improve your voice:

- Record your voice. That is how you really sound.
- Ask someone you respect for honest feedback.
- Speak from your diaphragm, not your nose or throat.
- When anxious, take deep, slow breaths and breathe in power while breathing out anxiety.
- Hire a voice coach. Voice is a very difficult thing to change without professional help.

*See* Image; Image – Body Language; Image – Dress; Image – Handshake.

# INFORMATION FLOW

## TO GET INFORMATION, YOU MUST GIVE INFORMATION

Respect the chain of command.

Make sure your superior has no surprises from your area.

Unless information is confidential, share it. People who feel included are more productive.

One of your main roles as a manager is keeping those above and below you informed.

Schedule regular or weekly meetings with all the people who report directly to you. This is an information exchange meeting and can take as little as ten minutes.

Write it down. For example: 'Tell Pat re: meeting Mon.' Things that are written are much less likely to be forgotten.

CYA (cover your backside).

*See* Memos/Letters.

# INTERVIEWING TO GET THE JOB

## DO IT RIGHT WITH THE FIRST COMPANY AND YOU WON'T HAVE TO DO IT AGAIN

Before the interview:

- Do your homework. Learn as much as possible about the company, the job, and the interviewer. Sources of information include newspaper articles, annual reports, the local business journal, the local librarian, and friends and acquaintances.
- Ask for a copy of the job description.
- Find out about the dress code. If necessary, drive to the company and observe people leaving work.
- When appropriate, put together a portfolio of applicable previous work (proposals, business plans, projects) and take it to the interview.
- Be clear in your mind why you're the best candidate for the job.

During the interview:

- Smile and greet the interviewer with a firm handshake and direct eye contact.
- Use the interviewer's name frequently. Don't use his or her first name unless you are given permission to do so.
- Never malign a prior employer or position.
- People like people they perceive to be like themselves. Search for commonalities.
- At the first interview, the purpose is to find a job skill fit. Questions about salary and fringe benefits are appropriate only in the final interview.
- Clearly demonstrate enthusiasm and a desire to get the job.
- An interview should be interactive. Don't dominate all the air time. Know how long the interview will last. Pace your answers for maximum information exchange in the allotted time.
- It's important to act as if you want the job. However, to keep yourself calm, remember you are deciding if you want the job too! Both you and the interviewer are assessing 'job fit'.
- Even if you're unsure at this point if you want the position, conclude the interview by clearly asking for the job. Your enthusiasm will be remembered. The interviewer has a gift (the job) to give. He or she wants you to want it.

Questions you should be prepared to answer:

- What would you like me to know about you?
- Tell me about yourself.

- What are your strengths and weaknesses?
- What did you like least and most about your last job and boss?
- Why are you looking for a job?
- Why do you want this job?
- Why do you feel you're the best candidate for this job?
- What are your long-term career goals?
- Do you have any questions about our company or this job? (*Make sure you do!*)

When answering questions:

- Be positive about yourself and your accomplishments.
- Always be honest.
- Don't point out problems or weaknesses that aren't brought up.
- If a weakness or problem is asked about, be brief and put as positive a spin on it as possible.

After the interview:

- The same day, send a follow-up note that includes:

  A thank-you for the interview.
  A summary of your strengths.
  Why you're the best fit for the job.

Call back, call back, call back. Pleasant persistence often gets the job.

*See* Hiring; Image.

# KEEPING UP TO DATE

Join and attend professional organizations.
Subscribe to trade-specific journals and magazines.
Read the business section of your local newspaper.
Subscribe to your city's business journal.
Read the *Financial Times*.
Listen to talk radio.
Buy motivational/instructional audio tapes for your
  car.
Network with people outside of your industry and
  company.
Watch television news programmes.

*See* Suggested Reading.

# LEADERS – TRAITS OF

Visionaries: See the big and future picture.
Inspire others. Use persuasion to help people see what's
   in it for them.
Lead through trust, not intimidation.
Consider their people their most valuable asset.
Know that valued workers are productive workers.
Lead by example.
Value innovation and creativity.
See change as opportunity.
Persist and believe in themselves and their mission.
Initiate; managers implement.
Are respected for their expertise.

*See* Managers – Good Ones.

# LISTENING

Listening is an extremely powerful skill. People will accept your ideas more readily when they feel you have truly listened to them.

Concentrate and focus your attention solely on the talker. Don't stare.

It's OK to take brief notes.

Listen with your eyes and ears. We believe what we see. Is the verbal and nonverbal communication congruent? Listen for what's *not* being said.

Don't interrupt. Listen to people all the way through to make sure you could repeat their point of view.

Maintain neutral body language. Avoid grimacing, shaking your head, and other gestures that will stop the talker. Encourage the speaker with head nods, uh-huhs, etc.

Suspend judgment about the person and issue. New good ideas often come from unexpected places.

You may want to paraphrase briefly what the speaker
  has said. Don't mind-read. If needed, ask for
  clarification.
Good managers are good learners. You're learning
  when you're listening.

*See* Body Language.

# MANAGEMENT BY OBJECTIVES (MBO)

## THE OBJECTIVE IS TO BE OBJECTIVE

MBO is a management planning and administration tool.
Supervisors and employees meet to set mutual, specific,
realistic, obtainable objectives.

Objectives are not the process but the measurable,
definable results. For example, it's not how many
sales calls you make, but how many sales you make.

Supervisors continually monitor and give feedback to
employees on how actual results are measuring up
to planned objectives.

MBO is then used in performance reviews. Evaluation and
rewards are based strictly on objective attainment.

MBO is a top-down objective-setting process. Upper
management sets corporate objectives first; then all
individual objectives must support corporate
objectives.

*See* Performance Appraisals; Total Quality
Management.

# MANAGERS – GOOD ONES

Praise in public, criticize in private.

Are even tempered and slow to anger.

Listen more than they talk.

Use the power of expertise often and power of position rarely.

Are consistent and fair.

Have a good sense of humour.

Are well organized.

Are decisive and open to input.

Build strong relationships.

Make expectations clear.

Practise excellent oral and written communication skills.

Delegate appropriately.

Explain why as well as what needs to be done.

Accept blame and share credit.

Face and resolve conflict.

*See* Leadership – Traits of; Listening; Power.

# MEETINGS

Before calling a meeting, explore alternatives:

- Can this information be handled without a meeting?
- Does this require consensus, discussion, or support?
- Could it be handled with a phone call or memo?

Purpose of meetings:

- To brainstorm.
- To give or exchange information.
- To make a group decision.
- To gather support, sell, or persuade.
- To motivate or inspire.
- To delegate or divide up responsibilities.

Planning an effective meeting:

- Write up and distribute an agenda covering these points:

Objective or goal of meeting.

Who will attend? There is a tendency to overinvite.

Participant preparation required prior to meeting.

Key points to be covered, time frames, and person responsible for each portion.

Logistics: date, start and stop time, and meeting location.

- Plan ahead for audiovisual needs and handouts.
- Determine ideal room setup to complement meeting purpose:
  Circle: brainstorming, giving or exchanging information.
  Conference table: decision making, delegating or dividing responsibility, *negotiating*.
  Classroom: informing, lecturing, motivating, or selling.

Conducting an effective meeting:

- Start and stop on time. Don't reward tardiness and punish promptness.
- Bring extra copies of the agenda. Having the agenda in front of participants will help the meeting stay on topic and on schedule.
- Stay in control of and stick to the agenda. When topics that are not on the agenda are raised, suggest adding them to the next agenda and move on.
- Review follow-up plans and assignments at the close of the meeting.

Tips:

- Consider starting at odd times – for example, 8:10 or 9:20. This tends to increase punctuality.
- Don't get caught in the one-hour meeting trap. Would thirty, forty, or fifty minutes do?
- Be prepared when asking for a decision. Identify key support individuals and possible obstacles through one-on-one conversations before the formal meeting.
- STOP side conversations by:
  Saying kindly – 'I'd appreciate your input. Is there something you're saying we need to know?'
  Stop talking and look at talkers. When they stop, you talk.

*See* Presentations.

# MEMOS/LETTERS

The goal in business writing is to be concise, clear, and
powerful.

Before you write, ask yourself:

- Why am I writing: to record, inform, ask, persuade,
  or justify?
- What is my goal?
- Who will be reading this?

Writing tips:

- Write the way you talk. Use the active voice. For
  example, 'I did', not 'It was done by me'.
- Use small, simple words. For example:
  'house', not 'abode'
  'and', not 'in addition to'
  'ask', not 'inquire'
- Use short sentences.

- Be neat and accurate.
- Bullet important lists.
- Use a positive tone as much as possible. For example, say what you *will* do, not what you *won't*.
- Avoid clichés, slang, profanity, and humour.
- Watch what you write. Once it's out of your hands, CONFIDENTIAL is only a request, not an enforceable command. If it's too sensitive, say it, don't write it.
- Don't write in anger. Give yourself overnight to cool off.

Memo/letter format:

- Many companies have preferred corporate formats. If yours doesn't, the following is a standard format.
State why you are writing. Grab the reader's attention here.
State the question, issue, or problem that needs to be addressed or solved.
Present the history or background information a reader needs to understand the subject.
Propose your ideas and offer suggestions for solutions.
Close by recommending the next step or proposing a plan for follow-up.

After writing, reread and ask:

- Does it flow?
- Are any important questions left unanswered?

- Is the tone as intended?
- Is the spelling and grammar correct? (*you're* spell check can't *due* it all.)
- What are the ramifications of misinterpretation?

After writing, edit for:

- Brevity.
- Clarity.
- Word clutter.
- Words that are used too frequently.

Finally, reread the memo/letter as if you were the recipient. If it's a *crucial* memo/letter, have someone else read and criticize it before it's sent.

*See* Presentations – Writing.

# Men/women at work

An awareness of how the opposite sex tends to think
and react will enhance your ability to be successful.
The goal is understanding and respecting the
differences. Both ways are valuable.
The following is a list of several different tendencies of
the typical man and the typical woman. They are
generalizations and obviously do not always hold
true. The most successful people are not typical.
Their behaviour is flexible and has a wide range of
options.

- Conflict:
  Men tend to confront and see confrontation as an
  arena for welcome competition.
  Women tend to avoid confrontation and prefer to
  defuse the situation.

- Decision making:

Men may seek information but tend to decide alone. Women usually prefer the consultative, consensus-building model.

- Mistakes, problems, failure:
  Men tend to blame the situation.
  Women tend to blame themselves.

- Help/advice:
  Men may ask for opinions or points of view but not 'help'. Men view asking for help directly as a sign of weakness.
  Women ask for it, seek it, and give it; at times, when it has not been asked for.

- Information:
  Men understand that knowledge is power and are quite cautious in what information they share.
  Women share information, sometimes too freely.

- Power:
  Men take and seek it. They see it as a positive.
  Women are more likely to align themselves with power than take it. They tend to share power.

- Praise:
  Men view the absence of criticism as praise.
  Women ask for it, seek it, and give it.

- Relationships:
  Men are self-focused and seek autonomy. They bond by teasing each other and participating in sports together.

Women are 'other' focused and seek connectedness.
They bond by sharing intimacies and vulnerabilities.

- Response to criticism:
  Men get angry and view apologizing as
  unmasculine.
  Women blame themselves and tend to apologize
  excessively.

- Response to feelings of others:
  Men experience discomfort and maintain a solution-
  oriented attitude.
  Women tend to be empathetic and listen.

- Style:
  Men are aggressive, competitive, dominating,
  control-oriented, and want respect.
  Women are nurturing, conciliatory, consensus-
  building, and want to be liked.

- Taking credit:
  Men take it.
  Women tend to share it or give it away.

- Talking:
  Men talk more, make more 'I' statements, interrupt
  more, compete verbally for air time.
  Women listen more, interrupt less, and ask more
  questions.

- Questions:
  Men ask how, what, where, why, when, and who.

Women ask how, what, where, why, when, who, and how do you feel about it.

Think of a continuum with MALE/MALE at one end and FEMALE/FEMALE at the other end. Most of us fall in the inner 50 per cent of the continuum. It's important that we become consciously aware of our reactions and behaviour and begin to choose what is best in the situation, not just react instinctively. Our head is on top so it will lead us around.

Obviously the best management style is a BLENDED MANAGEMENT STYLE.

*See* Assertiveness.

# MOTIVATION

Why motivate?

- Motivated employees are more productive employees.
- The first rule of motivation is to have clearly stated expectations.
- Tolerating poor performance is a demotivator both for the individual and for the group.
- People are motivated by having their specific needs rewarded.
- Possible needs are:
  Achievement.
  Affiliation.
  Attention.
  Autonomy.
  Belonging.
  Challenge.

Consistency.
Control.
Esteem.
Fairness.
Involvement.
Learning.
Money.
Power.
Recognition.
Respect.
Responsibility.
Security.
Self-worth.
Status.

Possible rewards: Remember, different strokes for
different folks. To be a reward, it has to be something
your employee values.

- Tangible rewards are external and generally come
  *after* doing the job. Examples are:
  Salary.
  Bonuses.
  Fringe benefits.
  Awards (pins, plaques, trips).
  Titles.
  Status (reserved parking spot, nicer office).
  Continuing education.

- Intangible rewards are internal and generally come
  while doing the job. Examples are:

Praise.
Responsibility.
Sharing your vision for your area.
Information.
Support.
Listening.
Autonomy.
Trust.
Input.
Feeling needed and that your job is important.

Motivation doesn't just happen, you have to work at it.

*See* Change; Difficult Irritating People.

# NAMES AND MORE

Keep a file of note cards or a computer file that lists
    personal facts about everyone you work for and
    network with, who works for you, your customers,
    suppliers, and so on.
Each file entry should contain:
    Name.
    Spouse's name.
    Children's names.
    Home address and phone number (for emergencies,
    sending personal notes, birthday and holiday
    cards, etc.).
    Special interests.
    Religious preference.
    Touchy subjects.
    Birthday, anniversary.
    Common interests and friends.

If these cards contain any sensitive information, keep them in a locked drawer.

*See* Names – Remembering.

# Names – remembering

When you're introduced, *listen* for the name.

Repeat the person's name immediately: 'Pat, it's nice to meet you.'

Say the name in your mind at least four times while looking at the person.

If you missed the name or were preoccupied, immediately ask for the name again.

Use the name at least twice more in the first conversation.

Write the name down as soon as you have a chance. If you are sitting around a table, write the people's names in the order of seating.

Make an association in your mind for the first name. The funnier the better; you'll remember it. For example: Cindy/sin, Pat/chatty patty, Jake/rake, Haley/daily.

*See* Names and More.

# New in Charge

Stop doing what your old job was. Learn to delegate.

If supervising former peers, deal with that issue head
on.

Go slow. Make no changes until you truly understand
the lie of the land.

Be low key.

Get clear limits of your authority from your new boss.

Get to know your new boss's style.

Ask lots of questions and listen, listen, listen.

Know you're in a honeymoon stage; everyone is on
their best behaviour.

Make no promises and few comments.

Meet with as many of your supervisees as possible to
get their ideas and suggestions and to let them get
to know you.

Manage by walking around; observe, observe, observe.

Don't let your new 'power' go to your head.

Cooperation and teamwork get the job done, not your power.

Assess:

- What are the problems?
- What are the strengths?
- Who are the key employees?
- Who has informal power among your employees, and how can you get them on your side?

Make sure you understand:

- The big picture and where your group fits in.
- Company values and goals.
- Company policies.
- What your boss expects of your group.
- Your group's history in the organization.
- What was liked or disliked about your predecessor.

*See* Change; Delegation; Listening; Managers – Good Ones.

# Office decor

Decide what you want your office to say about you and
decorate accordingly.

People will make judgments about you based on how
your office looks.

Not decorating says something too.

Before you 'decorate', check out the corporate norm.

Offices should be arranged to help you achieve
maximum performance.

Decide consciously if you want your office to be
inviting or not inviting.

- Chair(s) empty and inviting or stacked with stuff.
- A desk between you and empty chairs is a barrier.

Decorate to the next level to which you aspire.
Remember, your office is part of your corporate
image.

*See* Corporate Culture; Image.

# Open door policy

The *positives* of an open door policy:

- Encourages early awareness of problems and provides the opportunity to deal with them before they grow.
- Promotes a feeling of teamwork.
- Symbolically shows employees you care about them and will listen.
- Encourages hesitant employees to contribute.
- Keeps you in touch with the grapevine.

The *negatives* of an open door policy:

- Decreases your ability to manage your time.
- Frequent interruptions decrease productivity.
- Increases the likelihood of mistakes due to impulsive decision making.
- May encourage dependence. Employees aren't

forced to problem solve if you are always available to figure it out.

Suggestions:

- Designate and clearly communicate a daily quiet time within your area. Most interruptions come from peers and subordinates.
- If someone asks if you have a minute and you're really short on time, say 'Yes, just a minute' and stand up to have the conversation or say 'No, not now, let's agree a time to get together.'
- If all else fails and you need extended quiet time, find a conference room to work in and don't announce your whereabouts.

Cautions:

- If you never close your door, on that rare occasion when you do, your department will become temporarily nonfunctional trying to figure out what's going on.

*See* Time-Saving Tips; Time Thieves.

# ORIENTING
# THE NEW WORKER

Be prepared for the new worker's arrival: have the
work area set up, the phone installed, and so on.

Don't leave a new employee on his or her own the first day.
Assign someone to show the new worker around.

Assign someone to take the new worker to lunch and
generally look out for him or her the first week.

Much of what the new employee hears the first day will
be forgotten. Tell the person it's OK to take notes.

Clearly state performance expectations within the first
few days.

Orient the new worker to both the formal and the
informal written rules.

Make it clear who will be training the employee and to
whom to go for guidance.

Set a time at the end of the week to talk to the new
worker and review the week's experiences.

*See* Traits of a Good Employee.

# PERFORMANCE APPRAISALS

TO EVALUATE MEANS TO FIND VALUE IN

If you've been giving feedback all along, the annual
performance appraisal will be much easier.
Document and file this feedback as you go along and
compile it for the annual review.

A good performance appraisal is about motivating, not
judging. It should be an exchange. Listen more than
you talk.

Avoid last-six-weeks syndrome. Evaluate the entire
year's performance.

Give a written report to the employee prior to the
scheduled feedback interview. Be sure to focus on
behaviours, not attitudes. Be specific, give examples.

Rehearse the difficult things to say so you will be as
tactful as possible.

When you meet with the employee, stress his or her
strengths and make plans to correct weaknesses.

Set goals for next year. Finish the session on a
confident note about the employee's abilities.
If there is any reason to think that this employee may
be fired in the future, be very careful when you do
the review. The tendency is to be overpositive.
Remember, your goal is to motivate your employee. Be
clear about your assessment of his or her strengths
and weaknesses and help to set measurable goals for
the next year.

*See* Feedback; Goals; Listening; Management by
Objectives; Motivation.

# POWER

Power is the ability to influence others and outcomes.

There are two kinds of power: formal (positional) and informal (personal). Usually you must first have personal power to obtain positional power.

Formal power is your position or title within the organization. Using this formal, positional power is the least effective way to get things done.

Key ingredients to personal power are:

- Expertise and knowledge.
- Associating with powerful people and acting like them.
- Being decisive.
- Risk taking.
- Having a powerful image.
- For powerful body language:
  Walk assertively.

Stand straight.
Make eye contact.
Shake hands firmly.
Take up space.

Indicators of power:

- Title.
- Office.
- Access to people and information.
- Assignment to special tasks and projects.
- Respect from others.
- Opinion sought after.

Warning: Don't be fooled by titles. Secretaries frequently possess a great deal of power. To be powerful, you must have allies at all levels in the organization and network well.

*See* Assertiveness; Image.

# PRESENTATIONS – BEFORE

Ask yourself the following questions.

- What is the purpose of this presentation?
  To instruct?
  To inform?
  To entertain?
  To inspire?
  To persuade?
  To sell?

- Who is my audience and why are they here?
  Male/female/both?
  Old/young?
  Voluntary/required attendance?
  Superiors/peers/subordinates?
  What is their previous knowledge and/or attitude
  towards the subject?

Are there any big issues going on in this group that I should know about?

- What questions might arise?
- How large will the group be?
- When and where will I be making this presentation? FORMAL/INFORMAL SETTING? Before or after other speakers? Morning, afternoon, evening?

- How can I personalize the information to this audience and their interests?

*See* Presentations – Effective Writing; Presentations – Giving; Presentations – Reducing Anxiety; Presentations – Tips.

# PRESENTATIONS – EFFECTIVE WRITING

Know the answers to the questions posed in the
Presentations – Preparing section before you start
to write.

Write all the points you want to cover on 3 by 5 cards,
including jokes, stories, quotes, and facts. Use one
card for each point. Once all the information is on 3
by 5 cards, organize the cards and the flow of the
speech.

The three Ts of speaking are:

- Tell them what you're going to tell them.
- Tell them.
- Tell them what you told them.

Write in optional sections that you can add or delete
depending on whether you are ahead of or behind
schedule. (Your audience won't know the
difference.)

Write in the active first person – the conversational spoken word, not the written word.

The adult attention span is twenty minutes. Change your topic or pace every twenty minutes.

Use humour only if it is relevant and you are good at it.

Plan to use visual reinforcement of your message's key points. Use slides, video, flip charts, or overheads.

Close with a BANG – a quote, a call to action, a memorable story, or a brief strong synopsis of key points.

*See* Presentations – Before; Presentations – Giving; Presentations – Reducing Anxiety; Presentations – Tips.

# PRESENTATIONS – GIVING

## DON'T SPEAK TO THEM, TALK TO THEM

Immediately establish eye contact with the audience and smile.

Speak at a fairly rapid pace to keep the audience's attention. People speak at about 125 words per minute but have the ability to listen at a rate of 500 to 700 words per minute.

Use the podium as a base of power, authority, and control, not as a crutch to hide behind or lean on. Move away from the podium to warm up your audience or make the presentation more informal. Go back to the podium to regain control.

Punch your words. Vary your voice, tone, and pace.

Speak only after you have established eye contact with an audience participant. This will eliminate ahs, uhs, and nervous nonwords and help you avoid the swivel head syndrome.

Physically move from time to time but don't pace
about.

Use gestures. Be animated. Gestures should match the
size of the audience. The larger the audience, the
larger the gestures.

Signal the close. Say 'in closing . . .' or 'to sum up . . .'.

If you ask for questions and there are none, have one
closing thought prepared so you can formally close
on a positive note and won't be left hanging.

Be enthusiastic. Do anything, but don't be boring.


*See* Presentations – Before; Presentations – Effective
Writing; Presentations – Reducing Anxiety;
Presentations – Tips.

# PRESENTATIONS – REDUCING ANXIETY

## PUSH PAST THE FEAR. GO FOR IT!

Before the presentation:

- PREPARE, PREPARE, PREPARE.
- Know much more than you'll ever say.
- Memorize the first and last two minutes of your presentation.
- Audio- or videotape your practice presentation and watch it. It will increase your confidence. You're better than you imagine.
- Arrive early and mingle with the audience as they arrive.
- Check out the room setup, audiovisual equipment, lighting, and temperature. Minimize the opportunity for surprises.
- In the few minutes before you go on:
  Breathe in calmness, breathe out anxiety.
  Yawn.

- Visualize your audience enthusiastically responding. Remember, your audience is there to hear the message, not stare at you. Focus on the message. Pace if you need to. Your body may need to move. PRACTISE, PRACTISE, PRACTISE.

During the presentation:

- Remember to smile. It relaxes you and the audience.
- Pick out three or four friendly faces in the audience and look at them when you're speaking.
- Holding notes in your hand while you speak is acceptable.
- If your audiovisual equipment fails, turn it off and go on. Work on it during a break.
- Don't read your speech. If a word-for-word text makes you feel comfortable, keep it on the podium.

Handling hostile questions:

- Repeat or paraphrase questions in a more positive way. This gives you time to think.
- As you respond, gradually shift your body language and eye contact away from the hostile questioner.
- Continue with next point in presentation.

*See* Presentations – Before; Presentations – Effective Writing; Presentations – Giving; Presentations – Tips.

# Presentations – tips

THE MORE YOU SPEAK, THE BETTER
YOU'LL BE

Start and stop on time. Don't reward tardiness and
punish promptness.
Keep the room cool.
Don't apologize or make excuses. It decreases
credibility and brings the problem to the top of the
participants' minds.
Never say 'before we take a break'. You'll lose your
audience.
Audiovisual aids dramatically increase retention.
Don't give handouts before your presentation.

*See* Presentations – Before; Presentations – Effective
Writing; Presentations – Giving; Presentations –
Reducing Anxiety.

# PROFANITY

'YOU'RE D____ IF YOU DO AND
YOU'RE D____ IF YOU DON'T'

General rule: Don't use profanity.

If you don't use profanity, skip this section and try to be tolerant of others' use.

If you do:

- Be aware of whom you're talking to and who's listening.
- Be aware of 'acceptable' words in your company.
- Never, never write a profanity.

*See* Corporate Culture.

# PROJECT MANAGEMENT

THESE SKILLS ARE NEEDED WHETHER
YOU'RE ORGANIZING THE OFFICE
CHRISTMAS PARTY OR PUTTING A
MAN ON THE MOON

Have a clearly defined project description that outlines
goals, budget, and time line.

Divide the project into tasks.

Identify skills needed for each task.

Identify people who have those skills and get them
assigned to your project.

As a project manager, you are frequently dealing with
people you have no authority over, so your priority
at this stage is team building.

Develop a time line or flow chart with critical
milestone points that allow course corrections or
revisions; build in slush time at critical points.

Break the budget down by tasks.

Continually keep the project team aware of the big
picture and how the project is proceeding.

State emphatically to team members that you want to

be informed immediately if any task is not
proceeding according to schedule or budget.

Make yourself available to help when problems come
up. Don't shoot the messenger or after a while
there won't be any more messengers; they will come
to you only with good news information.

Continually monitor project progress.

Remember, as project manager, if all else fails, you need
to be prepared to do it yourself.

Celebrate project completion with the entire team.

*See* Managers – Good Ones; Teamwork.

# PROMOTIONS – HOW NEVER TO GET ONE

Worry more about getting your next promotion than
  you do about your current position.
Be a complainer.
Be a nine-to-fiver.
Be very moody and let it show.
Fail to respect hierarchy.
Don't adapt to your bosses' style.
Dress differently from the rest of the employees.
Talk about your personal problems too much at work.
Say 'That's not my job' frequently.
Frequently criticize your boss or company in public.
Highlight your deficiencies and weaknesses.
Act indecisively; use 'maybe', 'I'll try', and similar
  words a lot.
Whine a lot.
Refuse to be a team player.
Talk much more than you listen.

*See* Difficult Irritating People; Firing.

# SALES

Everyone is selling something: products, services, beliefs, thoughts, information. We're all trying to get someone to 'buy' or 'buy into'.

Think 'as if' you and the consumer are a team trying to meet the consumer's goals with your products.

Sincerely:

- Make your customers feel special.
- Find common ground. People are most comfortable with people like themselves; they like to buy from someone they perceive they have something in common with.
- Establish trust. Honesty builds trust.
- Use the customer's name and personalize the conversation.
- AT THIS POINT, don't mention the product. Your

109

goal here is to make the consumer comfortable with you.

Ask:

- Ask open-ended questions: who, what, when, where, why, and how?
- You're helping people make decisions. Find out what information they need to make a 'buy' decision.
- Discover the unmet needs/wants your product will fill.
- AT THIS POINT, your primary goal is to learn about the consumer's specific needs/wants so you can determine which specific product you're going to present to him or her.

Listen:

- Listen for what the buyer wants to know instead of focusing on what you want to tell him or her.
- Listen for key themes. What major factor does the buy decision hinge on? Examples of stated themes might be price, service, quality, exclusivity, durability, and reliability.
- Listen for the hidden agenda. What does your customer want emotionally? For example: to look better, peace of mind, prestige, a great deal?
- If more than one person is involved, listen for who will make the final buy decision.
- AT THIS POINT, you should clearly know what the

customer wants, why he or she wants it, and
therefore how to present it best.

Enhance:

- Present features and benefits of the product so it
  matches the consumer's needs and wants.
- Enthusiastically demonstrate a love of your product
  and a belief in yourself.
- Anticipate questions and objectives and have the
  answers ready. Complete knowledge of both your
  product and your competitor's product is critical
  here.
- At any point in this process, the sale may be made.
  Listen for buying signals. Don't oversell.
- AT THIS POINT, ask for the sale.

Sold:

- Ask for the sale.
- A key to closing sales is to be persistent but not
  pushy. It's not unusual to ask for the sale three to
  four times before the consumer makes a buy decision.
- If you get a NO, go back to ASK and LISTEN and
  gather more information.

The *Bullet Manager*'s method of selling is the *SALES*
method.

- Sincerely, Ask, Listen, Enhance = Sold.
- Selling is About Letting Everyone Succeed.

*See* Customer Service.

# SEXUAL HARASSMENT

The US Equal Employment Opportunities Commission (EEOC) defines sexual harassment as '*unwelcome* sexual advances, requests for sexual favours and other verbal or physical conduct of a sexual nature' when it is implied that failure to comply or tolerate the situation may jeopardize the employee's job status.

If you are sexually harassed at work, you need to make it quite clear to the harasser that the advances are *unwelcome*.

Make it clear to the harasser that if you are harassed again, you plan to report it to your boss and the harasser's boss.

Keep a log of comments and incidents with times documented.

You can do one or all of the following:

- Report to supervisors.
- File a formal company complaint.
- Contact the Equal Opportunities Commission (EOC).

If an employee reports sexual harassment to you, act immediately.

Ask the employee and document who harassed him or her, what happened, when it happened, whether it happened before, and what the employee would like you to do about it. Follow all company policies and report the situation to your supervisor and the personnel department.

Avoid sexual harassment charges by following these guidelines:

- Never touch an employee.
- Never tell dirty jokes.
- Ignore seductiveness from your employees.
- Don't use such terms as 'honey', 'sweetie', 'sugar'.
- Don't have 'dirty' books or pictures at the office.
- Don't talk about sex at the office.
- Don't make comments about an employee's appearance.

*See* Image.

# Smoking

If you smoke:

- In the 1990s, it's best to be a closet smoker.
- Smoking is now seen as a character flaw. People may draw negative conclusions about you based only on the fact that you smoke.
- Never smoke with a client unless you know he or she smokes. If the client does, go ahead and smoke; smoking together increases rapport.

If employees smoke, never state your personal opinion about smoking. If necessary, refer to company policy but stay out of this emotionally charged battleground.

*See* Image.

# STRESS

Facts:

- Stress is normal.
- Stress is contagious.
- Stress is increasing.

Four basic responses to stress:

- Resist.
- Avoid.
- Confront.
- Adapt.

Four common events that cause stress:

- Loss of control.
- Change (positive and negative).
- Feeling threatened.
- Unrealized expectations.

*See* Burnout.

# STRESS MANAGEMENT

IT'S NOT THE STRESS. IT'S HOW YOU HANDLE IT

Six steps to letting go:

- What things *must* I do?
- What should I do but others could do?
- What could I do but others should do?
- What must others do?
- What doesn't need to be done at all?
- Ask yourself: 'If all else fails, is it worth dying for?'

STRESS KILLS!!
Ten ways to deal with stress:

- Change the situation.
- Change your response to the situation.
- Ask yourself: 'What can I control? What's out of my control?'
- Delegate.
- Call 'time out'.

- Choose conflicts carefully.
- Practise positive self-talk.
- Talk it out.
- Learn to say no.
- Practise good habits in diet, exercise and the like.

*See* Assertiveness; Burnout; Conflict Resolution.

# SUCCESS

Successful people maximize their strengths and minimize their weaknesses.

Successful people see opportunity where others see obstacles.

Successful people:

- Are risk takers and enjoy a challenge.
- Are flexible and creative.
- Are decisive and tenacious.
- See mistakes as learning experiences. Win one, lose one, next one.
- Write down their goals and stick to them.
- Are curious and constantly learning.
- Are highly capable in their field.
- Have excellent written and oral communication skills.
- See the 'big picture' while attending to the details.

- Accept and use feedback to improve themselves.
- Are self-confident and use positive self-talk.
- Have a good sense of humour.
- Balance their lives and give themselves time for fun.
- Are energetic and enthusiastic.
- Surround themselves with positive, successful people.
- Are visible and present themselves well.
- Are psychologically resilient.

The more you have of the above qualities, the more successful you'll be. No one has them all.

Luck is a factor in success. However, successful people know how to maximize their good luck.

*See* Goal Setting; Image; Promotions – How Never to Get One.

# SUGGESTED READING

The following is a brief list of our recent personal favourites.

- All of *The One Minute Manager* books by Ken Blanchard and Spencer Johnson.
- *Claw Your Way to the Top: How to Become the Head of a Major Corporation in Roughly a Week* by David Barry.
- *Quality Is Free: The Art of Making Quality Certain* by Phillip Crosby.
- *The Seven Habits of Highly Effective People* by Stephen Covey.
- *Smart Moves* by Sam Deep and Lyle Sussman.
- *Swim with the Sharks Without Being Eaten Alive* by Harvey Mackay.
- *Working Woman* magazine.

*See* Keeping Up to Date.

# Teamwork

PICTURE THE CLYDESDALES. NOW
PICTURE WALKING SIX DOGS
SIMULTANEOUSLY. THE BENEFITS OF
TEAMWORK ARE OBVIOUS

Excellent teams:

- Start with a clearly defined mission statement that is shared by all team members. All decisions and plans relate directly back to that mission statement.
- Focus on work product and not personalities.
- Are both goal and process oriented.
- Discourage turf battles.
- Focus on the goal and not personal glory.
- Meet frequently and identify as a team.
- Resolve conflicts openly and quickly.
- Have an open flow of information.
- Discourage secrecy.
- Focus on solutions, not blame.
- Don't vote; build consensus.
- Celebrate successes and evaluate their failures.

Excellent team leaders:

- Share information freely, not just the what but the why.
- Are honest.
- Give both praise and nondemeaning, helpful criticism.
- Take part of the blame.
- Are enthusiastic.
- Have strong personal power.
- Never criticize one team member to another team member.
- Look out for their team members.
- Are good listeners.
- Make clear assignments of duties but encourage input outside of specific job area.
- May not always implement suggestions, but always encourage them.
- Empower team members.
- Have the ability to evaluate, react to, and defuse crises calmly.

Both team members and the team leader are loyal to the team.

*See* Brainstorming; Hiring; Project Management.

# TELEPHONE TIPS

THE TELEPHONE CAN BE YOUR BEST
BUSINESS FRIEND OR YOUR WORST
TIME MANAGEMENT ENEMY

First identify yourself.

Smile while you're talking.

Place your own calls.

Get to the point.

Don't use a speakerphone without permission.

Return all calls on the same business day or apologize
for your tardiness.

As much as possible, answer your own phone.
Depending on your business and for time
management purposes, you may want to have your
calls screened.

Picture the person you're talking to.

Minimize phone problems by:

- Returning calls at a specific time of day (bunch your
interruptions). The recommended time is just
before lunch or the end of the day. People are more

likely to be at their desks and more likely to be
brief and to the point at these times.
- Leaving a message with more than just your name.
  Include topic/purpose so the return caller will be
  prepared.

Call your own number periodically to see how and
how quickly your phone is being answered.

Reduce phone time by starting with 'I've only got a
minute but I knew your call was important and I
wanted to get back to you.'

*See* Listening.

# TIME-SAVING TIPS

Do it right the first time.

Decide which tasks you need to do an 'A' effort on and
which tasks need only a 'B' effort.

Discipline yourself to cut down on nonbusiness talk
and socializing.

Keep one task on your desk at a time.

Take the last half hour of the day to organize your desk
and plan for the next day.

Take something to read while you wait.

Leave detailed phone messages so that a response isn't
always required.

Delegate when possible.

When appropriate, make a phone call instead of
writing a memo or letter.

Start the day with a prioritized 'TO DO' list. A good
example is:

| Must DO today. | Must CALL today. |
| --- | --- |
| DO if time allows. | CALL if time allows. |

Set deadlines.
Use car time as think time.
Handle paper only once.
Use time-saving devices:

- Buy a good time management calendar system.
- Become computer literate and use your computer.
- Consider buying a car phone.
- Consider adding voice mail to your telephones.

*See* Open Door Policy; Telephone Tips.

# TIME THIEVES

Being too detail oriented or more detail oriented than the company norm.

Majoring in the minors.

Catching hot-potato problems – that is, catching problems your employees throw at you and taking charge when they are stuck. Give employees a few ideas on how to deal with the issue and then throw the hot potato back to them to solve.

Getting behind on the paper influx. Sort each morning into:

- To do today
- To do ASAP
- Later
- Trash or stash. (If you have trouble throwing it away, stash it.)

Not delegating.

Waiting.
Unnecessary conversations.

*See* Time-Saving Tips.

# TOTAL QUALITY MANAGEMENT

TQM (Total Quality Management) is an evolving management philosophy based on the following components:

Total:

- Refers to involvement and empowerment of all employees.
- Cross-functional and cross-departmental teams are used to assess and improve processes.
- Total external and internal customer focus.
- Value added in the eyes of the customer.
- System is totally data driven.

Quality:

- Meeting or exceeding customers' expectations.
- Doing it right the first time.
- Continuing evaluation and improvement.

- Focusing only on activities that add value to the customer and eliminating nonvalue-added activities.

Management:

- Top management is committed to TQM and understands that management-driven systems, not the individuals, are the problems.
- Focuses on How can we fix the system? not Whom can we blame?
- Uses the Plan, Do, Check, Correct system.
- Commits to ongoing training and education.
- Prioritizes all objectives and goals in terms of quality and customer focus.

The primary goal of TQM is to increase long-term profits by increasing quality, increasing customer focus, and decreasing costs.

*See* Customer Service; Suggested Reading (Crosby).

# TRAITS OF A GOOD EMPLOYEE

## A GOOD EMPLOYEE ALWAYS MAKES
## THE BOSS LOOK GOOD

A good employee:

- Is loyal and committed.
- Always attempts to see things from the company's point of view.
- Shares company goals and priorities.
- Is flexible.
- Is dependable; when assigned a responsibility, no one has to double check to make sure it's completed.
- Doesn't hide problems.
- Adapts to the boss's style.
- Takes initiative and follows through.
- Is self-motivated.
- Knows when to ask for help.
- Along with voicing complaints, presents solutions.
- Is a team player.

- Maintains a positive attitude.
- Has good self-esteem.

*See* Getting Along with Your Boss.

# Unions

Know exactly how your company's agreement with the union reads. If you don't know, ask someone who does.

Be familiar with all union policies and regulations.

Deal openly and honestly with the union.

Be clear on what issues you should handle and what issues should be referred to the union representative.

Maintain a good relationship with the union representative. Keep representative informed.

Attempt to resolve small complaints before they become grievances.

Never try to block a grievance.

Remember, the union is just as committed to the success of the company as management is.

*See* Conflict Resolution.

# ACKNOWLEDGMENTS

Harvey Mackay for, unbeknownst to him, giving us tremendous inspiration.

Adrienne Hickey for her kindness to us.

Stephanie Laidman for believing in *The Bullet Manager* and having the courage to go for forgiveness instead of permission.

Bruce Tracy for his speeding bullet style and for making it fun.

For information on speaking and training by the
authors contact:

On Target Training
3520 West 75th Street, Suite 201
Prairie Village, KS 66208
USA

# ABOUT THE AUTHORS

Pat Kaufman began her career as a psychotherapist and developed her expertise and interest in business as she became increasingly aware that many of her clients' problems centred on managing the personal/family/work balance. Still maintaining an active private psychotherapy practice, she also acts as a management consultant, focusing on beginning entrepreneurs and small or family businesses. Her clients have also included Fortune 500 companies. A popular speaker, she lives with her husband and two children in Prairie Village, Kansas.

Cindy Wetmore is the director of retail training and services and a project leader in the sales and marketing division of Hallmark Cards, Inc. Her experience also includes two years as an independent contractor for National Seminars, Inc., a public-seminar company, where she presented over 150 seminars throughout the United States and Canada. Continual requests from seminar attendees for concise, practical, how-to desk reference material led her to develop the idea for a book like *The Bullet Manager*. Married and a stepmother of two, she lives in Lake Quivira, Kansas.

# MOVING UP TO MANAGEMENT

Nick Thornely and Dan Lees

This is a first class handbook and practical guide for people on the first rungs of the career ladder. The most successful managers today think of themselves not as some kind of a policeman, but as team coaches – they care for their teams, look after their welfare, guide them and enable them to realise their full potential. *Moving up to Management* provides valuable insight into all aspects of modern managerial techniques and is packed with examples and illustrations from the many successful companies whose chief executives and senior managers have been interviewed by the authors especially for the book.

£6.99 Net in UK only

ISBN 0-09-941521-6

**NO HASSLE!**
**Taking the stress out of work**

Dr Sue Cartwright and Professor Cary Cooper

This invaluable book provides an entirely new approach to the ever present topic of stress at work. Instead of the usual advice about reducing the effects of stress on mind and body by healthy living and eating, it takes a far more positive and specific attitude. The authors, who both work in the Department of Organisational Psychology in the Manchester School of Management, examine various stressful situations and give solutions to them, ranging from dealing with difficult colleagues to crises such as mergers, redundancy, sexual harassment and ethical problems. The strains of interface between home and work are also explored.

£8.99 Net in UK only

ISBN 0-7126-5772-X

## PERFECT NEGOTIATION

### Gavin Kennedy

The ability to negotiate effectively is a vital skill required in business and everyday situations.

Whether you are negotiating over a business deal, a pay rise, a difference of opinion between manager and staff, or the price of a new house or car, this invaluable book, written by one of Europe's leading experts in negotiation, will help you get a better deal every time, and avoid costly mistakes.

£5.99 Net in UK only

ISBN 0-7126-5465-8

**THE PERFECT PRESENTATION**

Andrew Leigh and Michael Maynard

When everything seems to go right, you perform at your absolute best, your audience reacts enthusiastically and comes away inspired, then you've given the perfect presentation!

But success is underpinned by hard work, and the authors of this book provide the necessary framework on which to base your presentations, under the headings of the 'Five Ps': Preparation, Purpose, Presence, Passion and Personality.

Many major organizations have used material from the courses on which this book is based. Now you can gain those benefits – at a fraction of the cost.

£5.99 Net in UK only

ISBN 0-7126-5536-0

# PERFECT BUSINESS WRITING

## Peter Bartram

In every job, writing plays a part – and the ability to write well helps you to perform your job better. Good writing is important both for you and for your organization. It enables you to communicate effectively with your colleagues. It advances your career prospects. It contributes to the success of your company by improving communication with customers and suppliers – and it enhances the corporate image.

If you, like so many people, lack confidence in your writing ability, this book is the perfect answer.

£5.99 Net in UK only

ISBN 0-7126-5534-4

## PERFECT TIME MANAGEMENT

### Ted Johns

Managing your time effectively means adding value to everything you do. This book will help you to master the techniques and skills essential to grasping control of your time and your life.

If you can cut down the time you spend meeting people, talking on the 'phone, writing and reading business papers and answering subordinates' questions, you can use the time saved for creative work and the really important elements of your job. Learn how to deal with interruptions, manage the boss and cut down on meetings time – above all, how to minimize paperwork. You'll be amazed how following a few simple guidelines will improve the quality of both your working life and your leisure time.

£5.99 Net in UK only

ISBN 0-7126-5549-2